I0419708

Kangaroos
For Kids

Amazing Animal Books
For Young Readers

By
Rachel Smith

Mendon Cottage Books
JD-Biz Corp Publishing

Read More Amazing Animal Books

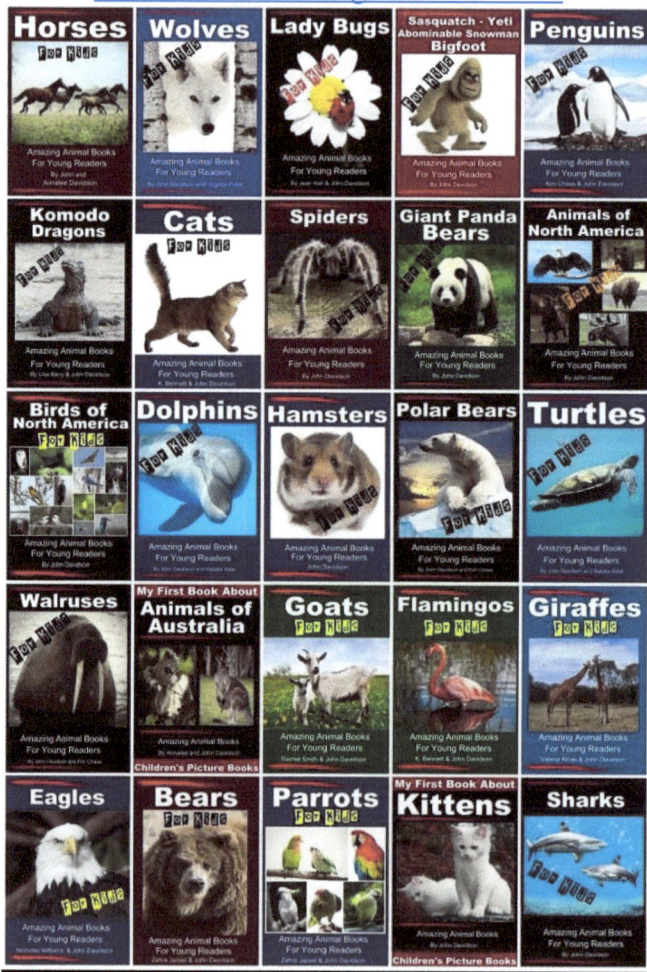

Purchase at Amazon.com

.

Table of Contents

Introduction

The kangaroo has long been a favorite animal of children everywhere. With its amazing way of hopping across great distances, and its kicking and boxing to defend itself, it's a unique animal through and through.

The reason they're so unique is that they are from Australia. Australia is a place with many unique animals, from the koala to the wombat to the dingo.

Kangaroos have long been a symbol of Australia, and it's no wonder people find them amazing. Kangaroos are truly unusual creatures.

What is a kangaroo?

A kangaroo is a member of the family Macropodidae, which comes from macropod, which translates to 'big foot.' The word kangaroo itself tends to refer to the biggest animals in this family, but scientifically, there are many other animals that belong.

A kangaroo mom with her joey.

Kangaroos are very strong animals; they have huge muscles in their tails and legs, which allow them to hop very far. However, kangaroos don't hop everywhere; they also walk normally, such as when they're looking for food. They have big feet, small heads, and much smaller arms than legs.

They are marsupials. This means that they are mammals who carry their young in a pouch on their bodies while they develop as babies. Most marsupials are in Australia, but there are a few in other places, for instance the opossum in North America.

Kangaroos are pretty unique when it comes to their babies' development. A mama kangaroo is pregnant for about a month, and then the joey exits the womb (a joey is a baby kangaroo). However, this baby is about the size of a bean, and completely furless, sightless, and only having tiny limbs. What the joey does is crawl through its mama's fur and into the pouch, where it latches onto a nipple and stays there as it grows.

This is similar to the opossum in North America.

Once the joey has grown big and strong enough, it will emerge from its mama's pouch. However, joeys stay with their mother for a while, going in and out of her pouch, usually to nurse or because they got frightened. Mama kangaroos reinforce the bond between baby and mother by grooming their joey. Joeys will nuzzle their mother's pouch to let her know they want to be let into it.

Kangaroos are not an animal you want to pick a fight with. As mentioned before, they are very muscular, though not particularly aggressive. Kangaroos may kick by using their strong tail as a balance, or they may box with their paws. Either is painful, and it's best not to mess with kangaroos.

The kangaroo's top speed is 44 miles per hour, roughly, though they can only do this for a short distance. Most kangaroos hop along at a speed of more like 15 miles per hour. They are the biggest animals to get around by hopping.

Kangaroos live in groups, usually of at least ten kangaroos. These groups are called mobs. Eastern Australia has larger and more stable groups, but since Western Australia is more arid (dry, less rain) it has smaller groups.

They can also swim, and when being chased by a predator, may end up going into water to escape. If the predator follows, the kangaroo has been known to hold its head underwater with its forepaws and drown it.

They eat mainly grasses and shrubs, and their stomachs are like sheep's and cows', meaning that they have more than one chamber. Humans only have one chamber, for comparison. They also chew cud. This means that they partially digest their food, spit it up in their mouth, chew it for a while, and then swallow it again. Cows do this as well.

A rare thing about the kangaroo is its teeth. It has chopping teeth in the front, since it's a grazer and that will cut the grass close to the ground. In the back, however, it has molars, and as it chews, it slowly grinds them down and then loses them; new molars come forward. This kind of thing only happens in manatees, elephants, and kangaroos. It's called polyphyodonty.

Kangaroos in a mob often touch noses and sniff each other. This is how they gain knowledge of the group, and who stands where in the social order. Because of this, there isn't a lot of fighting among the kangaroos to find out who's in charge.

Kangaroos mate in a way that's a bit different from other animals. A male will watch and smell a female, waiting to see if she's ready to mate. If she is, he approach very slowly, trying not to scare her; if she lets him, he licks and touches her a lot, and then they mate. After that, he moves on to the next female. Sometimes, males may fight over a female, but usually the bigger kangaroo is allowed to mate without a fight from the smaller kangaroo.

Sometimes, kangaroos fight. One reason may be to mate with a female, but this is usually only among the small male kangaroos. One reason both sexes fight is for spots at water holes. These are usually short fights.

Long, ritualistic fights occur between males. This is usually done after petting and grooming each other; it's sort of a sign of status, because big kangaroos may simply refuse to fight small kangaroos. They do a sort of boxing, in which they may hit with their forepaws or kick with their legs. Winners of the fights, which tend to end in one giving up or moving away, tend to prove themselves important in the hierarchy (who's better than whom).

What kinds of kangaroos are there?

There are several kinds of animals within the general group of kangaroos. The biggest four kinds are generally the ones called kangaroos, though the other, smaller kinds are just as related.

A kangaroo lying on the ground.

The smallest kinds are called wallabies, and these are often quite small. There are many kinds of wallabies, far more than there are kinds of kangaroos.

In between wallabies and kangaroos are wallaroos. These are any kind of a medium size that have not been defined as kangaroos or wallabies. There are also a number of them.

Sort of outside this is the tree kangaroo, the only one from outside of Australia. It lives in Indonesia, and unlike the others, who live on the ground, lives and climbs in trees.

These kinds will be thoroughly looked at in this book.

The four kinds of big kangaroos

There are, as mentioned before, four types of big kangaroos. These are the Eastern gray kangaroo, the Western gray kangaroo, the red kangaroo, and the antilopine kangaroo.

A red kangaroo.

The red kangaroo is the biggest kangaroo. It is also the largest mammal that lives on land in Australia, at least out of the native creatures, and it is also the largest marsupial. It lives in the less fertile areas, all throughout the mainland of Australia (meaning that it doesn't live on the islands, such as Tasmania).

Only the male red kangaroos are red, with the females being a blue-gray-brown sort of shade. They have rather square shaped muzzles (which is their mouth and nose area), and can see about 300 degrees about it, thanks to the positioning of its eyes. Kangaroos are prey animals, so it makes sense that they have wide peripheral (side) vision.

These kangaroos often come together in very large numbers. This can mean, in a place with a lot of food for them to eat, well over a thousand red kangaroos in one place.

There are no predators for the red kangaroo. Once, long ago, they had predators such as the marsupial lion and the megalania (a very large lizard), but this was thousands of years ago. However, their joeys are still in danger from dingoes and eagles. This is one reason mama kangaroos keep the joeys in their pouches.

While they do gather in very large groups for feeding, as more of a family group, red kangaroos keep things small, from two to four members, usually just mamas and joeys. But in areas that are more densely populated with kangaroos, they may stay in much bigger groups.

Red kangaroos fight like any other kangaroo, but there tends to be more wrestling involved, as compared to other species. The interesting thing about pregnancy with the red kangaroo is that the female is almost always pregnant; however, a mama kangaroo can sort of freeze a newly made baby in her womb while she waits until she is ready for the joey. A mama red kangaroo can have as many as three babies at once: a young one that can move about on its own but still nurses, a tiny newborn attached to a teat, and the baby she's frozen in her womb.

The Eastern gray kangaroo is the second largest kangaroo, and it lives in the areas that the red kangaroo doesn't, such as the East and South of Australia. They often stand over six feet tall; you do not want to mess with an Eastern gray kangaroo!

Their noses are different from a red kangaroo's, and they have fine fur covering them. An Eastern gray kangaroo is a light gray, almost creamy-colored in some cases.

Eastern gray kangaroos like wetter, more fertile areas than the red kangaroos, so this means that Australians, who tend to live in the wetter, more fertile areas as well, are more likely to encounter an Eastern gray kangaroo. It is nocturnal and crepuscular, which means it moves about and eats at night, dusk, and dawn. It eats mainly grasses, whereas red kangaroos eat a lot of shrubs and grasses.

The Eastern gray kangaroo lives in groups of 2-3 females, their joeys, and then two to three males; one of the males is always dominant. Female kangaroos tend to be very close to their female relatives, more so than towards males. Males don't help with the joeys.

The Western gray kangaroo has fur ranging from pale grey to brown. It is sometimes confused with the Eastern gray kangaroo in the places where their habitats overlap. They have sexual dimorphism, meaning that the two sexes look different; males are about twice the size of females.

This kind of kangaroo lives in groups of about fifteen. Only the dominant male in this group will mate with the females; this is decided through boxing.

There are two kinds of Western gray kangaroos: the mainland kind, and the Kangaroo Island kind. The Kangaroo Island ones live on an island called Kangaroo Island, named because they are everywhere on it.

For over 100 years, scientists weren't sure that there were two separate gray kangaroo species. Eastern and Western were easily mixed up with each other, and only in the 1990's did things finally get sorted out and the Western gray kangaroo recognized as its own species.

The antilopine kangaroo is the last type. This is the one that the least is known about. Its name means 'antelope-like' because it somewhat resembles an antelope. It is very large, near to Eastern gray and red kangaroos.

The history of kangaroos and humans

Kangaroos actually don't have a problem with humans at all; instead, it's the humans who may have a kangaroo problem.

A kangaroo enjoying being petted.

When the first humans to live in Australia lived there, the Australian Aboriginals (meaning the natives of the land), they relied on the kangaroo for a lot of things.

This included and still includes meat, hides, bones, and tendons, all of which were used to support themselves and for other functions. No part of the kangaroo was wasted; even some of its genitals (private parts) were used to make a ball to play a game with.

For the Aboriginal people, Dreaming is an important part of their culture; the kangaroo was a part of that, in some of the areas used for Dreaming.

When the colonists came, they also used kangaroos. They shot and ate them. Kangaroo meat is quite healthy, since it's very lean, meaning that it has little fat. The colonists also used the hides.

While the native peoples suffered, the kangaroo was only helped by the colonists. They cut down trees and made more grasslands, they cut down on the number of dingoes, and they added places with water in the arid areas. The kangaroos could spread farther than ever.

Nowadays, kangaroos are not endangered, and actually need to be culled every so often, which means that a number of hunters are allowed to kill them and possibly use their meat and hides. It's an over 200 million dollar industry in Australia.

Kangaroos are shy creatures, and will usually avoid humans rather than attack them. In older times, colonial Australians were known to keep them as pets, even in one case a kangaroo getting help for an injured owner.

The biggest problem for kangaroos that has to do with humans is getting hit by cars. It's a lot like the problem deer have in many countries with cars; these can do a lot of damage or even kill a kangaroo, because it gets dazzled by the car lights or something like that. Also, most animals just can't fathom something that goes as fast as a car.

Otherwise, however, the kangaroo generally has a fairly good relationship with the Australians.

Wallaroos

Wallaroos are the medium, or in between, sort of macropod. Their name is a portmanteau (meaning two words combined) of kangaroo and wallaby. Sometimes, the antilopine kangaroo is counted as a wallaroo, but it behaves very differently from the other two kinds of wallaroo.

A wallaroo sitting.

Wallaroos tend to hold their elbows against their bodies and keep their wrists raised. Their shoulders are also held back; these are things that kangaroos don't always do. They also have a black rhinarium; a rhinarium is a wet nose, like dogs and cats have. A wallaroo's is always black.

There are two kinds of agreed upon wallaroos: the common wallaroo and the black wallaroo. Both are thickset and solitary.

Common wallaroos come in four kinds, the main two being Eastern wallaroo (which is gray) and the Euro, which is more reddish. The other two live in very remote and small areas, and not a lot is known about them.

The black wallaroo lives in steep, rocky ground. It is solitary, very muscular and heavily built, and is remote. It is sexually dimorphic, meaning that the males are black and the females are more of a light gray. It is the smallest of the wallaroos, and very shy. Not a lot is known about it either.

Wallabies

A wallaby is a small macropod. There are many kinds out there, falling into about five or six categories.

An albino wallaby. Albinos occur in most kinds of animals, and it just means that they don't have pigment, or colors, in their bodies.

One type is the rock-wallaby. As you've probably guessed, this is a type of wallaby that lives in rocky areas. They live in steep and hard to reach areas. They are incredibly agile. This is their strategy to survive: hide in rocky, high, and hard to reach caves and such during the day, and then go out into the grass and such to eat during the night.

They may hide among boulders, or on cliffs. It depends on which of the many types of rock-wallabies they are. Rock-wallabies live in colonies, but males are fairly territorial, meaning they have their own area and they don't want other males to enter it. They don't mind females, however.

Rock-wallabies rarely venture far from their rocky homes.

Rock-wallabies are also endangered; they are extinct in some areas, and a lot of them are monitored by scientific communities. A lot of effort has been expended to try to save the rock-wallabies, but there are a lot of non-native animals that compete with it for food.

Pademelons, also known as scrub wallabies, are the tiniest kind of macropod. The name comes from a badly pronounced version of the Aboriginal word badimaliyan. They live mostly in forests, and they have thick, short, and almost hairless tails.

They live in dense forest undergrowth, or thick scrubland; pademelons make tunnels in the plants, and tend to hide. However, like the rock-wallaby, it faces problems from creatures imported to Australia from other countries: feral cats and dogs, plus foxes, are a constant danger to the pademelon population. Also, it has to compete with legions of rabbits for food, also an animal not native to Australia.

They used to be hunted a lot more for their meat, by both colonists and Aboriginals. Their fur is very soft, and their meat is said to be pretty good.

However, pademelons are doing a lot better than the rock-wallaby, and in some areas, they are hunted to bring down the numbers.

Next comes the dorcopsis, another member of the macropod family. It lives on various islands outside of Australia; it is also considered a wallaby, from the black dorcopsis to the white-striped dorcopsis to the brown dorcopsis.

Some live in New Guinea, some on Indonesian islands and others still on Papua New Guinea and West Papua. All this is in the same general area. The gray dorcopsis, which is only one of the dorcopsises hunted for its meat, is considered vulnerable, but the black dorcopsis is the most endangered.

There are also hare-wallabies, which looks similar to hares and rabbits in some ways. One prominent kind, which lives on two or three islands off of Australia, the banded hare-wallaby, has stripes, or bands, all across its body. They used to be on the mainland of Australia, but couldn't survive there.

Unlike kangaroos, hare-wallabies tend to be pretty aggressive, at least in the case of the males. Hare-wallabies hide in thick shrub and nest there.

Lastly, there is the average wallaby, which is most closely related to the kangaroo: these macropods are the Macropus genus. They looked the most like kangaroos too.

Tree kangaroos

Tree kangaroos are indeed kangaroos; they are just evolved a bit differently. They don't have the same feet of the kangaroo, and instead of hopping, they climb trees. They are the only members of the kangaroo family who truly live in and are adapted to trees.

A tree kangaroo.

It's said that the tree kangaroo evolved from a pademelon-like ancestor, the same as kangaroos in mainland Australia. However, when the area they were living in, New Guinea, ended up with a thick rainforest, they evolved over many years to be able to climb the trees. There are also some in far North Queensland, in Australia, but these also stay in the trees and are a fairly small population.

Tree kangaroo's feet are actually longer and broader than a terrestrial (land) kangaroo, and have curled claws to hold on to trees. They also have a sponge like grip on their paws and feet, which helps them hold onto trees. They also have a long tail, which they use for balance; they aren't able to use it to support their bodies in a fight the way kangaroos can.

Also, instead of sweating, they lick their forearms to cool off. Tree kangaroos are very slow on the ground, walking and sort of hopping along as fast as humans; because their tail is bigger than a terrestrial kangaroo's, they must lean forward to balance themselves. However, in the trees they are incredibly agile and fast.

Tree kangaroos eat mostly leaves and fruit, but will eat things like sap and baby birds on occasion. Their biggest threats right now are loss of habitat and hunting.

Conclusion

Kangaroos, along with wallaroos, wallabies, and various other macropods, are incredibly interesting animals. Due to mostly being isolated from other kinds of animals during their development, they're very different than the kinds of animals you might find in Europe, Africa, and continental Asia, even very different from animals in the Americas.

Hopefully, kangaroos will long be the symbol of Australia, and continue to flourish or do better in their habitats.

Author Bio

Rachel Smith is a young author who enjoys animals. Once, she had a rabbit who was very nervous, and chewed through her leash and tried to escape. She's also had several pet mice, who were the funniest little animals to watch. She lives in Ohio with her family and writes in her spare time.

Publisher

JD-Biz Corp

P O Box 374

Mendon, Utah 84325

http://www.jd-biz.com/

Mendon Cottage Books

P O Box 374, Mendon Utah 84325

Mendon Cottage Books

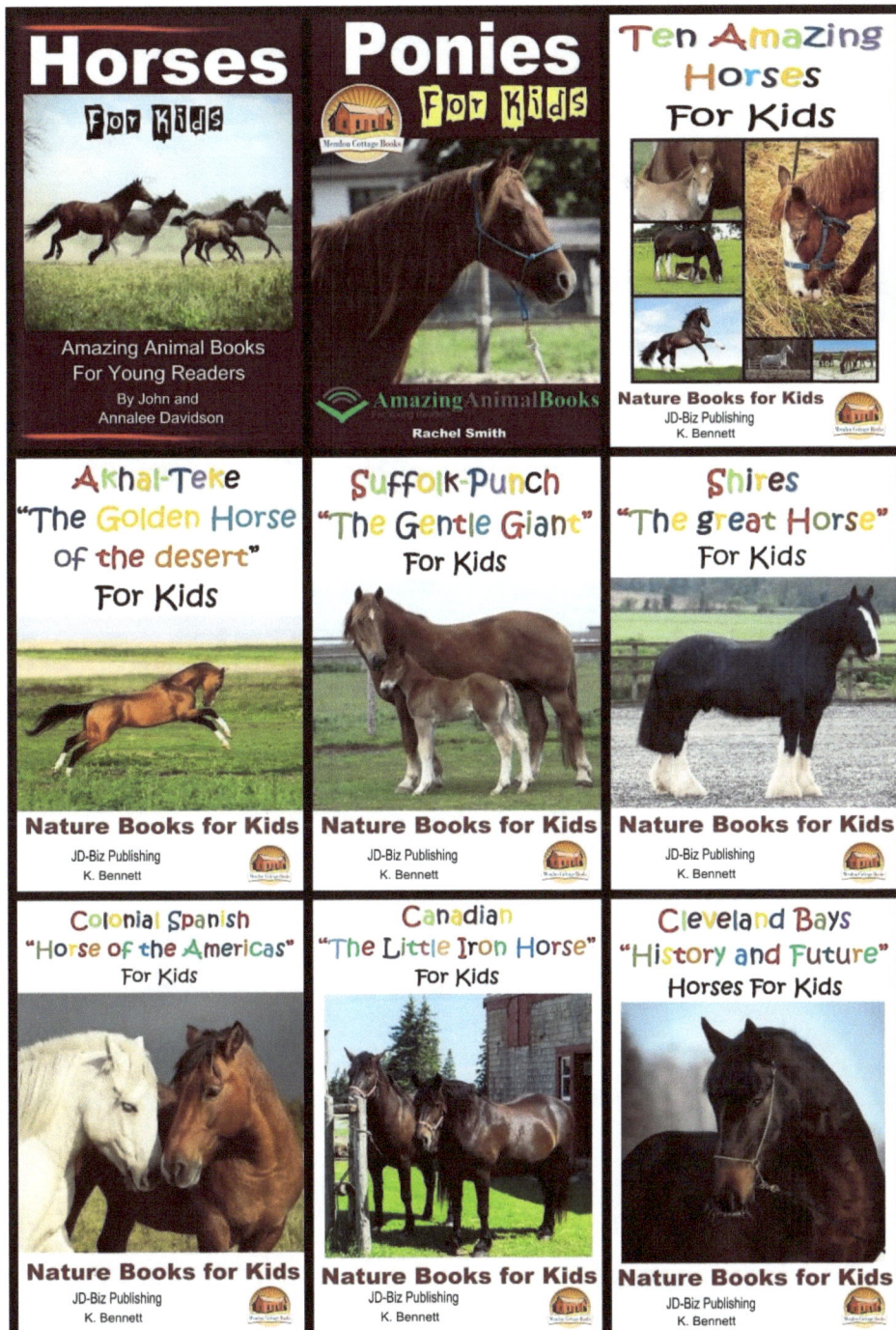

Top Ten Dog Breeds
For Kids

Amazing Animal Books
For Young Readers
Katie Bennett & John Davidson

German Shepherds

Dog Books for Kids
K. Bennett

Bulldogs

Dog Books for Kids
K. Bennett

Dachshund

Dog Books for Kids
K. Bennett

Poodles

Dog Books for Kids
K. Bennett

Labrador Retrievers

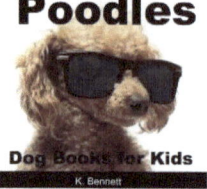

Dog Books for Kids
K. Bennett

Rottweilers

Dog Books for Kids
K. Bennett

Boxers

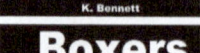

Dog Books for Kids
K. Bennett

Golden Retrievers

Dog Books for Kids
K. Bennett

Puppies
Dog Books For Kids

Amazing Animal Books
By John Davidson

Beagles

Dog Books for Kids
K. Bennett

Yorkshire Terriers

Dog Books for Kids
K. Bennett

Dogs
Top Ten Dog Breeds
For Kids

Amazing Animal Books
For Young Readers
Zahra Jazeel & John Davidson

Cats
For Kids

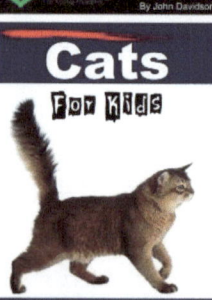

Amazing Animal Books
For Young Readers
K. Bennett & John Davidson

Foxes
For Kids

Amazing Animal Books
For Young Readers
Zahra Jazeel & John Davidson

Wolves
For Kids

Amazing Animal Books
For Young Readers
By John Davidson and Virginia Fidler

www.ingramcontent.com/pod-product-compliance
Lightning Source LLC
Chambersburg PA
CBHW050907290526
45792CB00002B/730